Poets' Corner
2021

The Bayside Writers' Group

Copyright © 2021
The Bayside Writers' Group
All Rights Reserved
ISBN: 978-0-6489459-5-6

This publication may not be reproduced, stored in a retrieval system, or transmitted in whole or in part, in any form or by any means, electronic, mechanical, photocopying, recording, or otherwise without the consent of the author(s). Inquiries should be addressed to the publisher.

Published in Australia
Printed by Ingram Spark

Poets' Corner 2021
Authors: Amanda Divers, Ann Simic, Judith Dowling, Lucy Tomov, Peter Levy, Rehaf Al Maalouf, Rose Crane, Roslyn Evans, Sandra G Lanteri, Suzanne Siebert.

Design: Sharon Hurst
Uploads: Alex Nutman a.e.nutman@gmail.com

Acknowledgements:

I would like to thank all those who took the time to submit their works to us, especially in these difficult times.

Please note that if anyone would like to make contact with any of the poets in this collection that the best way would be to either post a letter:

The Bayside Writers' Group
22 Stradbroke Avenue
Brighton East, Victoria, Australia 3187

Or email:
baysidewritersgroup@bigpond.com

Contents

Amanda Divers
- Combat 1
- Disillusion.. 14
- Effervescent 26
- Fight 32
- Siren song... 49

Ann Simic
- A chance meeting 2
- Exposure sites, 2021.. 15
- Hymn to Maria... 27
- Killing people off in English folksongs.................. 38
- Storm at Mornington Pier.................................. 50

Judith Dowling
- Bella Vista... 3
- A timely wedding 16
- Marigold's hope chest 28
- Ophelia's kitten 40
- Today or tomorrow 54

Lucy Tomov
- Airplane.. 4
- Fire 18
- Girl at the stoplights 30
- Kindness.. 43
- Little little 43
- Living thing... 51

Rehaf Al Maalouf
- The city of jasmine . . . Damascus 6
- Your smile that day 20
- It is just a picnic.. 45

Peter Levy
- Mrs Jones 5
- I bless you 19
- Freedom 31
- Contradictions 37
- Change 44
- I know you 44
- Thinking too much 52

Rose Crane
- People could be the birds 8
- Stick, stone and shell 21
- A gift to remember of a younger me 33
- Trams and wishes 46
- Wealth of play 56

Roslyn Evans
- The aviary 10

Sandra G Lanteri
- All in a day's work 12
- Return to the cathedral 22
- Water gardens 36
- Dark light 47
- Joe 57

Suzanne Siebert
- It is done in time 9
- Ode to the soul 24
- Hostage 34
- Divide 48
- Wood, water and betrayal 58

Combat

If tonight was the night
Blessed upon the world
My weary head would rest
Upon the sturdy shoulder of the universe
Oh to be a small dot
A small pigment of nothingness
A dime I am not, nor am I a rock
Smoothed out and shaped
A product of destruction
A love-struck apocalypse
Impish and headstrong
At peace I am not.

Amanda Divers

A chance meeting

Here and here, now and then, in my meanderings I scramble across a fabulous creature, a living being, a mysterious insect in the bush, bewildering, baffling, bizarre, whimsical and rare. I lift it on a leaf.

I scrutinise it. It ogles me back with its bold, beady eyes. It could fly away on its long gossamer wings, veined in intricate patterns. It stays as I steadily tread home.
I sit on a log in awe, staring. Its powerfully clawed front

legs like shovels. I imagine it, mole-like, burrowing in the underworld, eating roots, surfacing to mate in spring, responding to the loud, insistent male mating call.
How lucky, I think, that she allows me to gawk impertinently

when she has pressing generational matters to attend to.
I photograph her and post it. Monique, my clever niece tells me it's a MOLE CRICKET as I survey its cylindrical body bracketed by long levered back legs for powerful take-off.

Time to return her to the bush, thank her for letting me touch her wondrous world. I may never see her again but she will be there underground until the male rises from the depths and she joins him for a brief interlude.

Ann Simic

Bella Vista

They're building a box around the corner
'Bella Vista is coming down!'
It was Arthur Winter who built that elegant home.
His luck was in gold – in Sovereign Days
And is now turning in his grave
As he reclines in his final resting place,
Next to his wife and sons.
It you go to visit the cemetery –
If you sit and listen
You can hear him groan
While his wife is weeping.
His sons blaspheme, 'Too late, too bloody late,
Bella Vista is coming down'.

His great-great grandchildren
Will have but a strand of a story to tell
Bella Vista will fade away
Into a page of a musty book, never read,
Or perhaps stay in the minds of those who care
Enough to remember.
For the remaining span of their life.

They're building a box around the corner
And dividing that square into twelve
To the utmost height permitted.
The courtyards will have five pot plants each
Hiding behind bland walls
Money is happy. 'Who cares',
It yells, with all its might
'Bella Vista is coming down'.

Judith Dowling

Airplane

Cup me in your hands
and raise me to the sky.
Dressed in pink and white
feathers burning bones in place.

Jewels christening indents of skin
eyes are unfolded and golden
an animal blinking.

The parade is leaving,
balloons bursting
the colour leeches into my skin
and reflects upon the sea.

Lucy Tomov

Mrs Jones

White cliffs of shattered glass will fall as splinters must remain
In trust forever still part of something, partners to the grain.
No more than the child I see staring though desperate to be born
Within my eyes, to be saved, as if by me, to be touched, abused and torn.
How still the cliffs keep falling, Mrs. Jones has won this day
Or lost it through her fear of life, blessed in such full decay.
A word, a phrase, a look, she knows the art so well
The baby cries and growth goes down to sand, far lost within one's hell.
Excalibur emerged, I thank you mom, small room, lights out at seven
The baby feels the shattered glass, first step towards one's heaven.
I spin by chance the living wheel it always touches land
My cliffs had fallen long before, that beast could clasp this hand.
To look into the pain filled eyes of youthful sticks and stones
I touch those white cliffs standing firm, and curse all Mrs. Jones.

Peter Levy

The city of jasmine . . . Damascus

Oh poor Damascus . . .
The pure sounds became noisy
The pure air became dirty
The jasmine roses became tatty
The pure people became nasty

Oh poor Damascus . . .
Where are you? Take your sons back to the previous heavens
to the jasmine gardens, to an era before weapons
To an era before weapons

Oh poor Damascus . . .
Please don't be cruel . . . forgive who made you cry
In war there's no rule . . . open a new page please try.

Oh poor Damascus . . .
The authentic gorgeous bride . . . wear your wedding dress again
Your beauty is not acceptable to hide . . . dance romantically under the rain

Oh poor Damascus
I miss you, beautiful lady
I miss your elegance
Please call me when you are ready
To heal our wounds to make a difference.

Oh beautiful Damascus . . .
I am waiting to hear the pure sounds one day
I am willing to feel the pure breeze everyday

I am hoping to smell the jasmine perfume under the sun's ray.
I am looking to see the pure people on the way
. . . along the way . . . all the way.

Rehaf Al Maalouf

People could be the birds

Only if people could be the birds. How to be like the birds, wings spread far and wide, from expansive and higher plains they fly. To be free as if I had wings, so I could fly, that is how I would rather be at times.

Be free with your love my dear, for you are not caged, the bird would say because that is what is meant to be. Make accessible the doors of your heart, thought and place. For it is love and skilful means, wisdom and grace that opens the hearts of others, but always be wise of who you allow into your heart and mind.

With the Salute to the Sun, arms wide open as if they were your wings to receive the seeds that contain secrets to sustain you in this life. Oh, a message in a seed with thoughts of possibilities and peace. For the birds would rather see you happy and content with what is and thus that is the beginning of good to come.

How do the auspicious black shiny birds know, how do they know, because they told me so? The seeds, the grains of fuel, the energy it gives to unlock the seeds of better things.

Not only with their beaks they speak but also through their eyes, as they sit up high and look at the ones below for, they can see the good and the darkness of the minds of many of humans. So nice are the seeds with thoughts of possibilities and peace.

Rose Crane

It is done In time

"It's done."
I am silent in an instant, in an instance I have lost
Unkind effects affect me in ways that can't be measured by time,
And even then, as a consequence it is far beyond even mine,
I have lost a part of treasure, of a pleasure that has played its part
When somewhere is not 'anywhere' because I don't know where it wanted to go –
And all of nowhere stretches on beyond horizons own take of beyond the dark
Too far from myself, too far, and uneasily for far too long
It all feels like 'nowhere' with no rest place to find any space again
Where a cumbersome memory tries and takes on my mind
From every corner and surrounds on every plane,
A sort that time tries to move us along, far further inside
Beyond the ones we know and extending far,
far on from those
So, if I lost what I knew of anything and everything that I felt belonged
This heart isn't beating for a reason,
It's trying to catch its breath, breathing in, breathing out
And as it's done
It's only possible that it's beating
Because the treasure of another one is close

Suzanne Siebert

The aviary

The old white birds flutter
And perch feebly on thin legs
Or lie prostrate
On soft nests of straw and cotton wool,
Cocooned in forgetfulness or pain.
Some even move around
On motorized devices
Carving holes in walls,
Corners off doors
In vain attempts to fly again.

Migratory birds
With thick black feathers
Fly among them
Bringing scraps of food
On silver platters
Beside wine glasses,
A link to a life long gone.

Younger generations of native birds
Visit the aviary,
Quarantines permitting,
In a regular attempt to reconnect.
Fluffy white fledglings
Entertain the older birds,
Either as pictures on the walls
Or in the flesh and feather,
Darting round, pecking at bright objects
On the shelves in the cages.

Death's shadow dances in the motes
Caught between the curtains
In the early morning light.
Death sidles down to wheelchairs
Parked in the empty spaces
Where TV blares to vacant eyes.
Death squeezes between bandages
And deep purple bruises
On lacerated limbs.
Death recoils from the stench
In bedrooms of the incontinent.
Death catches petals as they fall
From Mother's Day chrysanthemums.
Death waits impatiently
That final consummation.

Roslyn Evans

All in a day's work
after Jacques Prevert 1900-1977

She got out of bed
prepared his breakfast
he ate
he left

she showered
did the washing
hung it out
vacuumed the stairs
cleaned the windows
mowed the lawn
feed the cat, the fish, the dog
she forgot to eat

she did the shopping
paid the bills
collected his dry cleaning
she forgot to eat

she rang his mother
she rang her mother
took in the washing
ironed seven shirts
organised his surprise party
the doctor phoned with results
she forgot to eat

She set the table
cooked his dinner
poured his whisky

He returned
he asked
What sort of day did you have dear?
Oh, the usual, she replied
That's nice dear
What's for dinner?
were the last words she heard

Sandra G Lanteri

Disillusion

Utter confusion clouds my mind's eye
A cotton candy life
And I slip
searching through the frames of worlds I'll never see
Arrogant illusions
Hold on to me
I can only hope to understand
Just let me breathe
I sit there silent
Cloudy disillusion
The clock tick tocking my mind away.

Amanda Divers

Exposure sites, 2021

Walking by the water at Lakewood,
we chance upon people smiling,
talking, spreading cheer behind
their masks, beneath the trees,

beside the lake where diverse ducks
dive and dabble, chase, strut and stroll.
Water birds wade in from far and wide
before renewing their mystical roaming.

Dogs, in all shapes and sizes, colours
and conditions, wag through tracks
strain at leashes, toward the oval,
where, released, they frisk and sniff.

Parliaments of magpies caw at each other as we rest on
enchanted logs, laughing, touching the tangled theatre
of the bush, searching the sun and blue-eyed sky.

Later we sit in the warming night, star-struck, small,
gazing into the conscience of our souls, receding into
ourselves to recall all those exposure sites imprinted on
our being.

Ann Simic

A timely wedding

They arrived in a train
From a barely-there place
Up in the wheat belt country
Three dusty hours away
To get married
As soon as they possibly could
Before the baby was born.
A lovely church wedding
Was always the dream
Of the sweet bride-to-be and her man.
A small wooden building,
Modestly steepled and painted white
On a rise from the creek
Shaded by gnarled peppercorns
Weeping willow trees
And sadly-forgotten gravestones.
Set just behind the town
The place where her parents had wed.
How she wept as she squeezed her handkerchief
When told the wedding couldn't be
Until ceremonial paperwork showed no impediment
And the banns had been dutifully read
Then indeed they may return
In no less than fourteen.

The wedding party arrived in a borrowed V8
Cranking up the hill
The mother of the groom
The bride's two burly brothers
The groom proudly wearing his digger's hat

The bride all in pink, her dress and gloves
A square of tulle pinned to her hair
Clutching some sprigs of golden wattle
Her man freshly picked down the way.
She cradled her baby, still in her belly
Its arrival overdue
Gingerly she walked to the altar
Although provided with a chair
She preferred to crouch on the carpet
Comforted by a cushion
And there her brothers attended her
By waving their slouch hats for cooling

The bride's birthing waters seeped
She groaned as each said 'I Do'
Then pain again as it was pronounced
That she was a married woman, a wife.
So for better or worse, in grimacing labour
She was placed into the car
For a rocky ride to the town's hospital
Where within a minute or two
A fine baby boy was born.

Judith Dowling

Fire

You looked at the fire
the way a mother looks at her son.
Cautious and hopeful and beckoning him
to turn his head further from the bracken of
her nothing
and closer to home.

You look at me like I could tie
your mellow body to the
backer rails enclosing the backyard
we first held hands in.
Like I would be the pity you use to hold up
your nothing
as it glistens against the swollen oranges,
threatening their branches.

And I am tired,
but the lawn swallows my heels.
As the sky pillows,
breathy and golden
marked
with the soot on your hands.

Lucy Tomov

I bless you

I bless you with forgiveness, and forgive you with my blessings
I can't take the road you're on, and you can't take mine either
You see the world as you see it, and I see the world from my eyes
I love you amongst other people and things as a father and human being
I wish you to know real love amongst other people and things too
You make a choice every second of every day with every breath
You then have to live with those choices, every day with every breath
My life will come and go in an instant, and will seem as if I never lived
Your life will live in me as long as I take breath, locked safe for eternity
My body will waste away to that of a crippled ant forever dependant
You will experience the same cycle of change, but at your own pace
There are no easy solutions, just as there are no problems without solutions
Every step you take in the wrong direction, requires two steps to return from it
I bless you with the wisdom to know the difference, and be content with your choice.

Peter Levy

Your smile that day

Your smile that day has melted the ice.
Your smile that day has thrown the dice.
My mind after that was a space of probability.
My heart since then became a collection of poetry.

With that smile,
You were the hope when there was no light
You were the only star in the heavy dark night.
You were the soft breeze that took my soul to the upper height.

Because of that smile
I conciliated with life and I gave it another chance
I ended the endless war; I gave away my lance
I celebrated the peace; I started to cheer and dance.
I announced the victory after the defeat, I felt the trance.

Oh, that smile . . .
Which returned me back to be a petite child,
who is always brave to love, with no way to hide,
who makes the whole world stands to her side,
who will find you wherever you are without a guide,
because . . . the moon always attracts the tide.

Rehaf Al Maalouf

Stick, stone and shell

The child does not know why it loves the things it does. Why it loves the stick, stone, and shell. For how does the child connect with nature and learn what it needs to learn from it? For the stick is not really a stick to the child. Is it a bat to hit a ball with or just something to hold? Anyway, they choose to make it whatever they want.

The stone that they touch and feel it in their hands with its ridges, colour, and texture and how calming that can be and from a place with memories of times past with experiences to hold and treasure. To feel and hear what the shell has to say. For they all have stories and secrets to share for the ones who dare to listen what nature and sea has to say. For that single object from the natural world that passes through its hands has profound wisdom and wonder. Where it has been and whose lives it has touched. I wonder what secrets they hold for the ones who understand. Such wisdom, such wonder in the everyday things of the natural alluring world.

Rose Crane

Return to the cathedral

After many years away
he walks the tessellated aisle
to the altar where he once served

Gothic windows allow summer light
glowing amber over mellow pews
The forest of marble pillars
not so easily absorbed, stand firm

fan vaulting insists on the divine
but the towering organ
the interweaving of man's brain and brawn
allows humanity entry

It's a measured welcome
the gestures are there to be read
as the child in him revisits
the familiar gold Duccio-like Madonna
eternally playing second fiddle to her son
the pious cherubs and stony-eyed saints
the spent candles of intercession
held tightly in brass
the lectern near the vestry door
empty of the printed truth
and the two purple velvet chairs
fit for a cardinal or a king
still pose pompously on the stage
giddy with entitlement

The air hangs centuries heavy
with dogma, ritual, misogyny, hyperbole
and much is needed to be said
but a rush of noisy tourists
assaulting the air with unseeing lenses
makes dialogue impossible

He leaves
man and boy leave
by way of the green fluorescent exit sign
fragile words unspoken
questions, forgiveness
unresolved

Sandra G Lanteri

Ode to the soul

Oh, my sacred soul, true compass amongst this world I remain held
Within
Your honest grandeur
I conserve myself as your servant for now and time beyond

Oh, my sacred soul, how you chose and deliver me; evolve my heart to a promise of salvation
Do you remain eternal as I see you be
Oh, yes, with pleasure I grant you to be
As you are more constant than my angels and gentleness I seek

Your privilege is but mine to share the sacred seal, vast knowledge beyond all spans, all season, all language, all personal sensation does not compare to this earthly reason

My reign, my master, my secured, my Divine and ravine, the chalice I drink from expels disdain or harbor of sin
Without you I am a clumsy observer, without your supreme lead

Oh, my sacred soul
You find myself in realms that I alone cannot reach
Challenge my steps purely,
To experience an endurance of all you lay at my feet

Oh, my sacred soul
As I walk upon the gravity of the earth to transpire,
deliver in kindness and faith

You tempt without sin, you excite creation and transpire
word and in story
Purest essence, precious listener where I begin

All is unseen, teaching in absolute protection
Allowing me complete submission to what lays beyond
Benevolence from all disturbance of thought
I am seduced under your reign

Oh, generous and sacred soul, I entrust my day,
my night, my sensation, my love, my delight, my
deliverance in what only can be granted by prior insight
takes me on

Suzanne Siebert

Effervescent

Whose heart is that? I don't think I know
Its owner is hostile and refuses growth
Dark decadence and a sour candied heart
Effervescent souls dancing in the dark
Twin flames that begin to shake
Ginger star seeds in galaxies far faraway
She gives her heart a shake,
And screams, "I've made a big mistake".
The only other sound's the break,
Of distant waves and birds awake.
Whose heart is that? I think I know.
Its owner is quite angry though.
She was cross like a dark potato.
I watch her pace. I cry hello.

Amanda Divers

Hymn to Maria

The blossoms still bloom at Maria's place though she
is no longer there, no more is she waylaying me as
I wander for a walk and a coffee. Last time she told
me in tears that a man set foot in her room at night –
opened the front door and befuddled her bed, breaking
bread; then five men, not touching her, just sitting there
and she, paralysed and petrified.
Now they've taken her away and I pass
her place in peace with a sigh that she is no longer free
to bother me – about her key not working or her TV,
her shadow life.
Now she must linger how long in one of
those homes, secreted away, to be safe.

Ann Simic

Marigold's hope chest

On her twenty-first birthday
Marigold's hope chest arrived
Boxed and bound by sturdy rope,
Protruding from the boot of the Austin A40.
Chinese! Shiny, carved and camphor oiled
For collecting all the things
A young lady could possibly need when she married.
Calendar tea towels from the nineteen fifties
Embroidered pillow slips and lace trimmed sheets
Dainty table cloths for dainty tea parties
A Robur tea pot to last a lifetime
And an array of dinner ware
That could be matched and added to
Over the years of matrimony.
It wasn't quite her pride and joy
But it certainly was her mother's
For come the day of Marigold's marriage
Its contents would be displayed in the front room
Along with the wedding presents
For the enviable viewing of family, friends,
Especially neighbours and in-laws

On her thirtieth birthday
Marigold received from her mother
A set of hand-crocheted antimacassars
To protect the three-piece suite
Her mother had planned for her
For many-a-year
And dear old Ruby from next door
Presented her with a set of bone-handled fish knives

Still in their box, in need of a polish
And a crystal jug with just the tiniest chip.
After she placed these things into her hope chest
She removed her most secret possession
From a box lined with fading pink tissue –
Her robe *du soir*, her negligee *a la fois*
Ivory silk and satin, lacey and long.
Ostrich feathering at the décolletage.
She held it against her body
Then slipped it over her nakedness
Unpinning her hair which fell to her shoulders
As she glided around the room
Enthralling her audience of one –
Her mirror.

Judith Dowling

Girl at the stoplights

With your hands tied
you look to me
like a prisoner of sorts.

You stand at the crossing
of two roads without mirrors.

Your hair streaming out
like
brushfire.

Watching time spin her web,
as the buzzing passes and passes and passes.

Lucy Tomov

Freedom

A whisper to no-one. I breathed it in
Freedom is everywhere.
A whisper to everyone. Trumpets shrill the air.
Freedom is within a grasp.
I look around me, blushed and in awe
Suddenly freer.
Smiling, my wants are for not one thing more
We are free.

Peter Levy

Fight

Selenite
Seldom quiet
My words, a sedentary break from your life.
Your lies ricochet
Like silver bullets with no faith
You are the shape of all my nightmares
The elusive silver lining of care
This silence screams and shouts
Toss me like a river cling to me with doubt
My hand is on the trigger. Baby take me out
Listen to the wind storm
Listen as it screams
Have you ever wondered what it all means?

Amanda Divers

The gift to remember of a younger me

Winter days outside when the days were cold. How to keep warmer, happier, and bold. So, I had to find a way. Oh, the joy of a challenge to find a way. Winter came and a pile of chopped wood delivered to the owners of a little house, the little house I grew up in, with had a wooden stove, a driveway without a car.

The wood was there for the necessity of survival. Wood to burn, to heat the food, to nourish the souls, to keep us warm for when the sun choice not to shine.

The pile of the chopped wood would bring for me joy and a challenge. For how I would love to climb it, to go faster and harder. As the days went by, I could see the pile of wood get smaller which made me a bit sadder.

Having to wait a few months till the next pile of wood to be delivered, for how I like to climb and have some fun. In the meantime, to find new challenges just as rewarding or even more. Oh, the joy of a challenge.

Now 30 years on and how lucky I am, for across the way, piles of wood that look like little hills for me to climb. Allowing myself to be the child for just a while that likes to climb and see how fast I can go. A gift placed there for me, is how I choose it to be, as it reminds me of a younger me so I can be more of me again whenever I choose.

Rose Crane

Hostage

There are times I've been held hostage by my own submission, overruled
Neglected, unforgiving emotions abuse me internally because they can
Even my own silence harasses and taunts me and keeps me in suspense
Waiting and daring apathy to keep me here and then malignantly advance
What then, predict a violent null and void prospectus, possibly with no chance?
When I revisit conversations, migraines begin their chase, vibrating in my veins
There's no place for light, or gleam, or shimmer, no people, no plans, no sound
Only a reluctant, damaged desperate cry, hiding at the back of my mouth;
But why should I give it the breath it needs when there is no beating heart?
It's parched for thirst of reason, undeniably left unquenched for hope
To explain the losses taken away before they even came, for reasons of their own
Failing that there is nothing to regale for and that will never be relieved,
As a hostage, does one surrender, by choice, by disillusion or by despair?

Perhaps life made broken promises and then just left them there
Yielding to be close, to just be touched with something to believe
By providence I'm alive, but opportunity has failed to come
Give me mercy, give me strength, and just give me something good
I'm still asking for that needed breathe to be released and to be understood

Suzanne Siebert

Water garden

Morning, noon, and night
but I could be exaggerating
my Grand-mother loved to water
or, to be more precise
loved to drown her mainly asphalted garden

sometimes I would follow
as she drowned the old fig tree
silky-eyed begonias
open-hearted geraniums
and pink faced daisies
before having a good go at the
giant monstera deliciosa
whose sprawling tendrils
would one day grab and gobble up
my four-year old self

In my brash twenties, for a bit of fun, I joked
You do know all your watering
has sexual connotations, don't you?
A widow for many years
she pursed her lips into a rosebud
as I have seen her great-grand-daughter do
and blushed me a you know who smile

Needless to say
there are always daises, begonias and geraniums
in my well-watered garden
but monsteras I leave well enough alone

Sandra G Lanteri

Contradictions

My life is full of contradictions
No single thing could ever define me
One day at a time is all I can manage
Pressure keeps me blind when I should see.
Questions of my past are always haunting
Reminding me of good and bad I've done
So easy to forget or change the details
To win the losing races I have run.
Underneath my world is empty
Victories are but few and far away
Whenever love comes knocking in the darkness
Younger hearts will always win the day.
Zealots live and die in silence
Always first to make their stand
Believing in the world the way they see it
Courageously committed to this land.

Peter Levy

Killing people off in English folksongs

Sing a song of death in ditties
and all the mysteries they hold-
those old folksongs of Limeyland
riddled through with woes.

And every way those songs portrayed
how people perished tragically-
the words pluck at our heartstrings
and leave us crying happily.

Most perished of a broken heart
as all good lovers do
though I've always found hearts
go on beating even in a stew.

Too many seem to drown and die-
they probably couldn't swim;
why didn't someone tell them
not to jump in on a whim.

Cruel wars claimed quite a few
which hasn't altered much-
silly men are still out there,
dirty guns held in their clutch.

Hanged for being a highwayman
was another way to go-
in songs it sounds romantic
but in life it isn't so.

A certain few were stolen by the
good old Queen of Elfland-
a strange, improper way to hide
death by an evil hand.

Some wandered off into the woods
and lost, lay down and died-
funny, when I walk in woods
I don't just groan and die.

A person mistaken for a swan
by a trigger-happy hunter-
only a fool would believe that one
I couldn't be much blunter.

'Cos humans look just like a swan-
someone should have shouted, "Duck!"
Instead they're standing petrified,
crying, "Oh my god, oh f ... shucks".

Ann Simic

Ophelia's kitten

Ophelia's flying plaits swooped up, down and over
Above the fence line of my house
I knew by the squawks, the squeaks and hisses
By her huffing and puffing as she tried to sing
That she was jumping again – on her trampoline
Then no sound until she knocked on my door
'I've come to tell you something important.'
Her little body was doing little girl half jumps
With hands clasped together at her chest
Her mouth displayed burgeoning new teeth.
'I want you to get a kitten. You really need a kitten,'
She announced, 'Because you're lonely'.
She wagged her finger at me so I copied her petulant pose
'No I'm not, yes you are, no I'm not, yes you are,' we argued
'In a week. You simply must get a kitten in a week'
I nodded no as she nodded yes
In two weeks then! .'
It was settled for her, but not me.

At the end of Ophelia's fortnight's allotted time
She knocked at my door again
Did you get it? Get what? The kitten!
– Thoughts of cats having far escaped my head –
Her flushing face drooped into a pout
Her shoulders dropped to a slouch
There was no kitten in my arms, nor smooching at my heels,
Nor one in a box peeping, nor purring on a bed of sunlight

So, of course, she started to cry
'You're just like my mother', she stamped the ground
'My mother hates cats.
I wished and I wished I could share one with you
I really hoped you were so lonely and needed a cat
But now I can tell
You're not nearly as lonely as me.'

A year passed by
Tilly the Tabby arrived next door
Ophelia's teeth had grown perfectly straight
A thick bob replaced her plaits
And she insisted her name was now Filly
Because, she said, it rhymed with Tilly
Though I rarely saw Tilly on four feet
She seemed to thrive in Filly's coddling care
A substitute brother and sister
Until one day it was time to wander . . .
The knock on my door was louder, more urgent
Tilly was missing, last glimpsed at my gate,
Into the vast unknown world next door
Through her tears Filly repeated over and over
'My darling baby has gone for ever'
The saddest of all words to hear.
Together we watched, waited and worried
Listened for sounds in the shrubs,

For a kitten crying in pain
Or maybe sounds of wild boar grunting
Such was the state of poor Filly's mind
She was silent. She held up her hand
To silence me when I spoke,
So stealthy, her movements
How concentrating was her expression

Then lying on her belly on my shallow decking
With one eye flat to the deck
She whispered, to me 'Be silent'
She had seen a small light, then two . . .
Two beautiful cat's eyes,
Staring, surrounded in blackness.
For a long hour she lay there
Refusing cake or juice for herself
Though she agreed to a morsel of sardine
To gently cajole Tilly to the small gap where she'd entered
Next, when I looked up from my gardening nearby
Everything was quiet except for lullaby humming.
Little Ophelia was holding her precious kitten
She'd been patiently, gently, rescued from that dark gap
She was safe!
I bent to touch them, to stroke Filly's hair
She shrugged away from me
And buried her face in the tabby fur
I knew it wasn't my place
It wasn't my place
Sadly
It wasn't my place
She moved away, out of my sight
To sit in a soft old garden chair
Enveloped. Away from me
And when I looked up again, they were sleeping.

Judith Dowling

Kindness

Her light falls in snippets of shadow,
through the cracks of a window pane
and from holes in the heavens.

She cradles love as though it built the Gods
winding herself around whispering clouds
around colour and sunshine and
the hallowed beauty of growing things.

All of which came from her.

Lucy Tomov

Little little

Take comfort in your smallness.

Let its silks drape over your shoulders
swathed in suns you will fade.

Oblivion's arms will catch your breath
and whisper sweetly in foreign tongue.

Till you sleep,
forgotten at last.

Lucy Tomov

Change

I feel that change is in the air
This privileged life is about to end
Maybe I won't be around when it happens
It is waiting, close, beyond a bend.
Where money has no value
Survival for the strong
Death on every corner
Nothing right or wrong.
Words will cease to be important
Humanity will hold the key
The blindness lifted from our eyes
To be what we will be.

Peter Levy

I Know You

To fly through the clouds, as I do, knowing little of them
I am a part of the crowds each day, but know less of them
The thoughts of my closest friends and family sometimes eludes me
But is it not funny, that on seeing you once . . . I know you.

Peter Levy

It is just a picnic

Whether the sky is cloudy, or if it is sunny
Whether you are poor or you have money
Whether it is misery or tastes like honey
It is just a picnic.

Even if the days become a little bit tough
Even if the ocean's waves get high and rough
Keep steering the ship. Never say I had enough
Face the storm with courage, face it with a laugh
Because it is just a picnic.

Sometimes you fall after climbing the rock
Or you believe in truth while it is a mock
Climb it again, and on the peak drink a glass of bock
To find the fact, break the cuffs open the lock
It is your picnic.

Spend it with love and give it a smile
Walk it with passion mile after mile

Open a new chapter and throw the black file
Human's life is short, it can disappear in a while
So do not be sad, do not be hectic
Because life is just a picnic.

Rehaf Al Maalouf

Trams and wishes

On the tram I sit. Out the windows the fellow travellers look. They look to the horizon sky.
Is it a memory of a distant land that they are looking at or just thinking that? Is it a hint of a place, warmer, lighter, and brighter?
Is that what they are looking at or do I just want to think that? Maybe that is what I would rather look at and think it to be.
An invitation came, from the distant land with words kind and caring bringing answers to solve some problems. It was speaking of new ways of being and thinking.
Who speaks these words to me, are they from distant shores or are they from my mind?
So, I look at the strangers on the seats, looking, thinking of their dreams and hopes of how they wish it to be.
They look tired of the questionable behaviour of others at work or home.
So, in silence they would look to the horizon sky which looks ever so far away and make the decision to find a way, how to find a way.
For their hopes and dreams for their lives and all while escaping with their minds on the trams while making their wishes.

Rose Crane

Dark light

Fuel fraught with anger, pride, hurt
he storms from the pub
to drive hard
the mountain road

sudden winter rain on snow
slants silver shadows over sense
and a missed turn
challenges clarity

the weariness of choice
go back, go forward
or soar with the gothic ghost gums instead
reach for the moon
Become a legend at last

Sandra G Lanteri

Divide

There are several different reasons that our paths collide
And others that just make our hearts divide
Eventually you take a thought, have a notion, and create a reason
For our friendship to sink and hide
Biggest overture is that you make it, break it, and then you cry
The barrel of your heart, scraping at the sides
To rid the development, with all its blame inside
Then you let me in for a moment, to tell me of December –
Then no other calls were made
Your decision, your path, your journey, your disclaimer
Disconnected us with your ego, to become the tides sailor
The leader of the severance and of the divide
And now you ask me why?
Do I not want to know?
Yet you shove it before my face when I have clearly said to you, "No"
No, I will not listen to the lot as a favour to you
To hurt me even more, with the degrader, its just going to abuse and act as saviour,
And suffocate me at the same time
Stick to your side of the great divide
Judgement only sits on one side, and it's sitting right next to you

Suzanne Siebert

Siren song

Shadows dancing intertwined
Moon light captures the sea
Stolen lullaby's from long, long ago
Sand pools in wayward palms
slowly drizzling away
Chaotic winds change
Cat like curiosity
And playful bright eyes
A siren like smile
The renegade defied
Perched upon a rockpool
bathing in the moon light

Amanda Divers

Storm at Mornington Pier

The gale-lashed pier at Mornington
heaving waves dashing its battlements,
plumed spray whipping mighty planks
as I scamper swathed in Arctic garb.

Four boys play in spindrift paradise,
bikes abandoned in favour of furious foam
and peril, to romp and caper on the high
winds of exhilaration, fish and chips forgotten.

A man of many years slips and falls
in the fury. They rush to his aid,
"Are you all right?" "Are you sure?"
He reassures them as he rises, smiles

upon their bright, warm-blooded, breathless
care, and continues his grind against the gale.
The boys hurtle, holler, sure-footed on the
slimy surface, the sea-fret, murk and mizzle,

belch joy into the wind and waves. The
heavy swell tickles the gurgling underbelly
of the boards, howls and shrieks its power,
eyes anchored on boats tossing turbulently.

While a few kids ride waves of freedom
escaped from warm, protective homes,
and a few older, rip themselves from couch-
potato Olympics to dare the elements.

Ann Simic

Living thing

Chaos seeps into love,
like blood into open air.

It is brazen and sweet

forbidding
us from crawling
back into the womb.

Warm
Scarlet
Dampness

isn't that all we're made of?

Lucy Tomov

Thinking too much

I often get the feeling that I'm thinking too much
That the real essence of life is simplistic
Concerns of the mundane will always be there
Are they real? Does it even matter?
In the scheme of things we are transient
We are bored by what we know
We are troubled by the insignificance
We think there must be more to it.
From one day to another, one week to another
The sameness of being is visible everywhere
What more is there to think about then?
Religion? Country? Earth? Cosmos?
Illogical beliefs are the faith of many
Desperate attempts to put a label on things
A reason for everything
A truth to hold onto as we slip further into the abyss
Planning for a future that will be what we hope for
Coping with the reality of now
Exhausting monologues in our brain that keep looping
Depression and meaninglessness? Maybe?
Are we being productive or not? Does it matter?
Have we executed our tasks correctly?
Will we be noticed in the rush to the finish line?
Is there some way of avoidance we can implement?
Yes, I think too much. But that's what I do.
Problem equals solution. Conflict equals acceptance.
I sometimes ponder what and why I think what I do
Why do I persist with the same baggage?
Is it *the devil I know* syndrome?
Do I find some solace and innate enjoyment in it?

I'm not sure. I'll have to think on it.
Maybe it's just a waste of time? My time at least.
I might protect myself from one or two calamities
Not the final one though.
The assault on our brains from everywhere is relentless
People I don't know or even care to know speak to me
Apps on my phone, emails and twitters, chatter away
I'm sure my mind has some saturation point
And it's the speed of things that's worrying too.
Too much too fast with too little time to check them
Nonsense becoming familiar and then true?
Pictures and projections that suddenly appear.
Will this war against my sanity ever end?
I yearn for peace at all costs. I don't care anymore.
I yearn for kindness and understanding and clarity.
Is that too much do you think?

Peter Levy

Today or tomorrow

This day is wet underfoot and graveyard grey
Is this today or tomorrow?
All doors are locked, welcome mats are sodden
Nobody will knock. They mustn't. They wouldn't.
Out in the hollowness people travel incognito class
Equalized, with faces masked, sinlessly shopping
Expertly weaving to keep apart
Wearing last night's trackies
Dark hoodies pulled up around the head
Hair jutting out at all angles
Gatherers and gleaners, we venture out
For staples we need, and no more
Showing only eyes, with deepening wrinkles, dark circled
Hands sanitised, knuckled fists on guard
Grasping shopping trollies.

Is that my neighbour under there ? Head down
I see him and he sees me, we don't quite see each other
Are we friends or foe? You just never know
The mystery lady at the counter says, as always,
"Have a nice day" and I say, as always, "You too"
When really I mean please, please don't die.
I drive home . . . the long way
The window screen is fighting a battle with the rain
The wipers incessantly arching , trying, trying
Non-stop . . . like heroes.
In the aftermath, the trees gently weep
The dog walkers leave their shelters.

A man is clearing a gutter
A woman is standing statue – still in the street
Looking long at a house she has passed many times before
Perhaps she is waiting for spring bulbs to appear
Perhaps because there's no hurry
Or perhaps she has lost her mind.

Judith Dowling

Wealth of play

A gentle boy that liked to play. His best friend that lived not so far away. They would fish together; play together and mostly they would have fun together. Billy carts they made of wood, wheels, and steering wheels. Comparing, showing pride in what they made to friends and others. My brother always looked forward to the ride in his billy cart. Eagerly he would wait from the push by his friend or sisters, that would start the ride he would enjoy on the road on the quieter part of town.

Sure, they would dare one another who could go faster, as friends do. But always healthy competition, never the comparing of who was better. All for the fun of the wealth of play to see how fast they could go and sometimes race they would with their hand made billy carts of wood, wheels, and steering wheels. He loved the days of play with his friend and billy cart. Memories that sustained him through times of worry, such pleasure he would find in the wealth of play.

Rose Crane

Joe
b. c 1897 d.14 May 1927

My name's Joe Lynch
Long ago
on a starless night
I disappeared
from the drunken frivolity
on a Manly-bound ferry

Vanished, I did
into an azure-blue melody
near Bennelong Point
weighed down by pockets of beer
and beautifully choreographed
some would say
I am my own cartoon

today ferries arrive, depart
from the crowded Harbour
and yes, I'm still here
my once colourful life
writ large into cultural legend no less
courtesy of Slessor
my good drinking Mate
who was always a sentimental soul,
and then by Olsen, on Opera
with his artful brush and living paint

Good lads
Pen and paint have kept me alive for you to know
I owe them both a beer.

Sandra G Lanteri

Wood, water and betrayal

The callous betrayal of your love has been made true
By your actions, lack of word, and made more than skin deep
The splinters, crafted to splint
The roughness, demanding to scar,
The drowning with intent, washing away any last hope to have your care bestowed upon me even when I choke
The collection of three
All demeaning and carefully bespoke.
I tore under the skin, I despaired on the dry granules of coldness of 'life giving',
And I was torn in the flesh by the harshness of your own felt deal
Can I appeal to the factors to change their actions, when the wood, the water, the rash all came together as one?
Is it even possible to heal?
There is little to think
I cannot survive on water I cannot drink, dried with salts that turn my flesh pink,
I break by the force of natures own strength
That even when hollow, I will inevitably sink
The wreckage I am came by your hand, of all three by your desired command

I won't remain in your directed custody or resign or fold
I am leaving the forces to have their redemption to
burn you, welt you and scold
Yet I am ready to return this inability to feel
To the devil as he's told and has already got a gripping
hold
I leave this burden, upon you even if it is never
unresolved

Suzanne Siebert

www.ingramcontent.com/pod-product-compliance
Lightning Source LLC
Chambersburg PA
CBHW010244010526
44107CB00061B/2671